D0548852

Profiles of the Presidents

ULYSSES S. GRANT

★ ★ ★

the Presidents

ULYSSES S. GRANT

by Jean Kinney Williams

Content Adviser: Division of Interpretation, Ulysses S. Grant National Historic Site, Saint Louis, Missouri

Reading Adviser: Dr. Linda D. Labbo, Department of Reading Education, College of Education, The University of Georgia

COMPASS POINT BOOKS MINNEAPOLIS, MINNESOTA

Compass Point Books
3722 West 50th Street, #115
Minneapolis, MN 55410

Visit Compass Point Books on the Internet at *www.compasspointbooks.com*
or e-mail your request to *custserv@compasspointbooks.com*

Photographs ©: Corbis, cover, 3, 40, 57 (bottom left); North Wind Picture Archives, 6, 10, 12 (top), 14, 17 (right), 21, 24, 29, 36, 42, 45, 54 (left); Oscar White/Corbis, 7; Stock Montage, 8, 11, 13 (top), 18 (all), 26, 33, 34 (bottom), 38 (bottom), 47, 58 (left); Hulton/Archive by Getty Images, 9, 13 (bottom), 15, 16, 20, 22, 25, 27, 28, 30, 31 (all), 35, 37, 38 (top), 41, 43, 49, 50, 54 (right), 55 (right), 56 (right), 57 (top left), 59 (all); Bettmann/Corbis, 12 (bottom), 19, 55 (left); Library of Congress, 17 (left), 32, 56 (left); Medford Historical Society/Corbis, 23; Image Courtesy of The Currency Gallery, 44 (all); Union Pacific Historical Collection, 57 (right); The Denver Public Library, Western History Collection, 58 (right).

Editors: E. Russell Primm, Emily J. Dolbear, Melissa McDaniel, and Catherine Neitge
Photo Researcher: Svetlana Zhurkina
Photo Selector: Linda S. Koutris
Designer: The Design Lab
Cartographer: XNR Productions, Inc.

Library of Congress Cataloging-in-Publication Data

Williams, Jean Kinney.
Ulysses S. Grant / by Jean Kinney Williams.
v. cm. — (Profiles of the presidents)
Includes bibliographical references and index.
Contents: Early days—Successes and failures—From store clerk to General—The White House—Gold, not greenbacks, and scandals—Life after the White House—Glossary—Ulysses S. Grant's life at a glance—Ulysses S. Grant's life and times—World events—Understanding Ulysses S. Grant and his Presidency.
ISBN 0-7565-0265-9
1. Grant, Ulysses S. (Ulysses Simpson), 1822–1885—Juvenile literature. 2. Presidents—United States—Biography—Juvenile literature. 3. Generals—United States—Biography—Juvenile literature. 4. United States. Army—Biography—Juvenile literature. [1. Grant, Ulysses S. (Ulysses Simpson), 1822–1885. 2. Presidents. 3. Generals.] I. Title. II. Series.
E672 .W727 2002
973.8'2'092—dc21 2002003035

Printed in the United States of America.

Table of Contents

★ ★ ★

From General to President

★ ★ ★

It was the winter of 1857, and the man huddled on the Saint Louis street corner was a sad sight. Standing next to the stack of firewood he was trying to sell, he pulled his coat closer in the wind. He was a struggling farmer, trying to earn money selling firewood. If someone had told that man he would be a national hero in ten years and well on his way to becoming president of the United States, he might have thought it a cruel joke.

U.S. Grant, the Civil War hero

His leadership in the Civil War (1861–

1865) made Ulysses S. Grant a hero on par with George Washington and Abraham Lincoln. The Republicans asked him to run for president. Grant was a modest man with neither the desire nor the disposition to be a politician.

A portrait of Grant with his wife, children, and grandchildren, taken two years before he died

He dearly loved his wife and children, however. Grant had struggled to support his family before the Civil War. Being president, he thought, would allow him to support them well. He also felt bound to do what he could for America after he had fought so hard to win the terrible war between the North and the South. As a war hero, he easily won the presidential election.

During the Civil War, Grant had risen quickly through the ranks to general. Both his troops and President Abraham Lincoln liked and respected him for his fearless determination in battle.

Ulysses S. Grant was the eighteenth president of the United States.

Grant was not nearly so bold and fearless in the White House. It was a difficult time to be president. The Civil War had only recently ended. Relations between the North and the South were still bitter. And the tide of violence against African-Americans was rising in the South. Historians have never questioned Grant's honesty, but he often showed bad judgment. As president, he surrounded himself with

men who became involved in scandals. In the end, he was not the strong leader his country had expected him to be.

After Grant left the White House, he lost all his savings when a business partner stole company money. Before he died of throat cancer after a long illness, Grant enjoyed one last success—writing his **memoirs.** His tale of fighting the Civil War sold well enough to provide for his wife long after his death. His memoirs are considered a masterpiece in military history. Ulysses S. Grant, a great general and a flawed president, has a secure place in American history.

▲ *Grant's love of cigars would cause the cancer that killed him.*

Early Days

★ ★ ★

Hiram Ulysses Grant was born on April 27, 1822, in a small white house overlooking the Ohio River in Point Pleasant, a village in southwestern Ohio. His parents, Jesse Root Grant and Hannah Simpson Grant, called their first child Ulysses.

In 1823, Jesse and Hannah moved slightly west to Georgetown, Ohio. Eventually they had three daughters and two more sons. Jesse ran a successful tannery that made leather out of animal hides. Ulysses was a quiet, calm boy. He developed a strong love for animals, especially horses. Young Ulysses became a skilled horseman and loved the outdoors. He

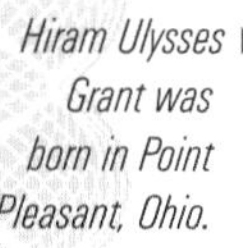

Hiram Ulysses Grant was born in Point Pleasant, Ohio.

hated working in the tannery, so his father often let him do other chores.

Hannah and Jesse Grant

In 1839, Jesse wrote to his congressman. He asked the congressman to recommend that seventeen-year-old Ulysses be admitted into the United States Military Academy at West Point. Ulysses was accepted.

At West Point, Ulysses discovered that his congressman had given his name as Ulysses S. Grant. The congressman had assumed that his mother's maiden name was Ulysses's middle name. In any case, Ulysses preferred the new name because he feared being teased about his actual initials: H.U.G.

At West Point, as expected, Grant proved to be a remarkable horseman. But in other ways, his four years at West Point were not notable. Few people would have predicted a great military career for Ulysses.

The U.S. Military Academy at West Point was established in 1802.

Grant as a second lieutenant

Grant grew 6 inches (15 centimeters) while at school, reaching a height of 5 feet 7 inches (170 cm). He graduated in 1843—a handsome and sturdy second lieutenant in the U.S. Army.

Grant was sent to an army post in Saint Louis, Missouri. One of his West Point friends, Fred Dent, came from Saint Louis, and Dent suggested that Ulysses visit the Dent family there. Like Ulysses, Fred's younger sister Julia enjoyed the outdoors and loved riding horses. Ulysses fell in love with Julia, but war would soon force him to court her long-distance.

Julia Dent

James Polk, the eleventh president of the United States

At that time, Texas still belonged to Mexico. In 1836, Texas broke away from Mexico and declared itself to be independent. Both the United States and Mexico wanted Texas. When U.S. president James Polk took office in 1845, he claimed that Texas was part of the United States. Polk sent 3,000 soldiers to Texas under the leadership of General Zachary Taylor. Ulysses Grant was among them.

The American soldiers were told not to start the fight with the Mexicans. Instead, they were to wait until the Mexican troops fired first.

In the spring of 1846, Taylor's troops traveled along the Rio Grande—the river that separates Texas from Mexico. Grant enjoyed the scenery and the warm weather and was thrilled to see a huge herd of wild horses. In April, when the Mexican army finally fired upon the American troops, the U.S. Congress declared war on Mexico. The pleasant scenes soon turned bloody, and Ulysses Grant got his first taste of war.

The battle of Chapultepec was one of the many of the Mexican War (1846–1848) in which Grant was involved.

Successes and Failures

★ ★ ★

At Palo Alto, Texas, the U.S. troops faced a Mexican army twice their size. General Taylor was confident, however, that his men had better weapons, and the Americans attacked.

Zachary Taylor (center) became the twelfth U.S. president, but died only sixteen months after his election.

General Winfield Scott

As quartermaster, Grant was in charge of the company's supplies. He was drawn to the fighting, however, and he soon discovered he had the nerve for battle. Grant stayed calm as the men around him were blown to pieces. On his own, he led a group of men in a charge against the Mexicans, capturing several prisoners.

Meanwhile, General Winfield Scott led another American army into Mexico, and Grant was soon sent to join Scott's men. As Scott's troops fought their way into Mexico City, Grant again proved his talent. He was promoted to first lieutenant. Among others praised for their bravery was Robert E. Lee. One day, Lee would find out how determined a soldier Ulysses Grant was.

The Mexican army finally **surrendered.** As the peace talks dragged on, the U.S. troops remained in Mexico. Far from home, Ulysses often thought about Julia Dent. He wrote to her, "You can have but little idea of the influence you have over me, even while so far away."

Grant proved his talent as a soldier once again at the capture of Mexico City.

Territory acquired by the United States as a result of the war treaty

In February 1848, Mexican officials agreed to a treaty. The United States got Texas, and the land that would become California, New Mexico, Arizona, Utah, Nevada, and Colorado. Mexico got $15 million.

By August 1848, Grant was back in Missouri, where he married Julia. He remained in the army as a quartermaster, and the happy newlyweds moved to army posts in Michigan and upstate New York. After his success in the Mexican War, Grant had high hopes for his future.

The next decade brought difficult challenges for the Grants, however. Their first son, Frederick, was born in

Frederick Grant

May 1850. Then, in 1852, Grant's army unit was transferred to the West Coast. This meant sailing to Panama (in Central America), marching across Panama, and then sailing up the Pacific coast. Julia, expecting their second child, stayed behind with her family.

When he arrived in California, Grant learned that he had been transferred again—to Fort Vancouver in Oregon Territory. There Grant's troubles really began. The fort was a lonely place, and Grant missed his wife and children terribly. His second son, Ulysses Grant Jr., had been born in July 1852.

Ulysses Grant Jr.

Grant's army salary wasn't enough to support his family, and he tried several ways to make extra money. He grew potatoes to sell to settlers who had just arrived in the territory, but many other people were doing the same. Grant lost money on other failed projects, too, and he became very depressed.

"You do not know how **forsaken** I feel here," he wrote to Julia after another transfer—this time to Fort Humboldt in northern California. Grant needed to be near Julia and the children. He grew even more sad and lonely. Many people think he began drinking heavily. In time, Grant realized that he had little hope of supporting his family on army pay. In 1854, he left the army and went back home.

Nellie Grant, pictured at age 9, was the Grants' only daughter.

Ulysses and Julia had a daughter, Nellie, in 1855, and another son, Jesse, in 1858. Grant enjoyed his children. He was a loving

Hardscrabble, the Grant family home in Saint Louis County, Missouri

and playful father. He would often wrestle with his children on the floor.

The Grants lived on land given to them by Julia's father as a wedding gift. But Grant had no more success farming in Missouri than he had in Oregon. In 1856, he built a house he named Hardscrabble on his property. It looked rough, but Grant was proud that he'd built it himself.

For a time, Grant added to his farming income by selling firewood in Saint Louis. Then, Grant worked for Julia's cousin in a Saint Louis real estate office. He hated collecting rent from people who couldn't afford to pay it, and he was not a natural salesman. Finally, Grant's father offered him a job in his leather-goods store in Galena, Illinois. In 1860, Grant moved his family there. The work did not interest him, but at last he had a steady income.

All this time, tensions between the Northern and Southern states were growing. Northerners and Southerners argued bitterly over slavery and whether it should be allowed in new states and territories. After Abraham Lincoln, a Republican, was elected president in 1860, some Southern states began leaving the Union. Eleven of them formed a new nation they called the Confederate States of America, or the Confederacy. War was just a matter of time.

The first shots of the American Civil War were fired at Fort Sumter in South Carolina in April 1861. Ulysses Grant left his father's store to sign up with the Union army. He never looked back.

The Grants lived in this Galena house after the Civil War.

The General

★ ★ ★

Grant felt very strongly about preserving the Union. He didn't think the Southern states should be allowed to withdraw from the United States without a fight.

The Union army needed officers. Because of his experience in the Mexican War, Grant was made a colonel. He led an Illinois **regiment** to Missouri in June 1861.

Grant had become friends with Congressman Elihu B. Washburne, who was also from Galena. Washburne recommended that Grant be promoted to a higher rank. By August, Grant was a brigadier general. He hired a staff of assistants, including another good friend from Galena—John A. Rawlins.

John A. Rawlins ▸

Although Grant had little success in the business world, he knew what to do when it came to war—go after the enemy. He did that from the start.

In February 1862, Grant led his men into battle at Fort Donelson in Tennessee. During the fierce fighting, Grant calmly encouraged his soldiers as he rode among them on horseback. Finally, Confederate general Simon Bolivar Buckner (whom Grant had known at West Point) sent a message to Grant. He wanted to discuss terms of surrender. "No terms except an **unconditional** and **immediate** surrender can be accepted," was Grant's now famous reply. U.S. Grant earned the nickname Unconditional Surrender Grant and was promoted to major general.

President Abraham Lincoln was disappointed in some of his other Union generals, but he soon learned Grant's value in the war. "I cannot spare this man. He fights," Lincoln said of Grant.

General Simon Bolivar Buckner

Confederate gunboats passed through Vicksburg, Mississippi.

And fight he did at Shiloh, one of the Civil War's deadliest battles. It took place in April 1862, along the Mississippi–Tennessee border. In this brutal, bloody battle, Grant's 60,000 men faced 40,000 Confederate troops. The Southern troops had surprised Grant's troops, and at the end of the first long, desperate day of fighting, Grant's men had been forced back. The next day, however, Grant's army regrouped. By nightfall, they had regained all the ground they had lost on the previous day. Now they were back where they had started—but at a terrible cost. Each side had lost thousands of men. "Oh God forever keep me out of such another fight," wrote one Confederate soldier. It was clear that neither side would win an easy victory in this war.

Grant next set his sights on the Confederate base of Vicksburg, Mississippi. From Vicksburg, the Confederates

General Grant leading his men in the Battle of Shiloh

were able to control the Mississippi River from New Orleans, Louisiana, to Memphis, Tennessee. A Union victory at Vicksburg would shatter that control.

Vicksburg, surrounded by swamps, was a difficult target, however. Union troops tried many times before finally taking it in July 1863. In that same month, General George Meade won a bloody three-day battle at Gettysburg, Pennsylvania. It had been a good summer for the Union army. Grant had regained control of the Mississippi River in the west. In the east, Meade had stopped a Confederate attempt to invade the North.

The Union army, led by General Meade, triumphed at Gettysburg in a battle that turned the tide of war against the Confederacy.

After another victory at Chattanooga, Tennessee, Grant was seen as the Union general who could defeat the South's military hero—General Robert E. Lee. In the spring of 1864, Lincoln promoted Grant to lieutenant general. He was the first person to hold this rank since George

Washington in the Revolutionary War (1775–1783). Grant now commanded the entire Union army. It was time to go after Lee's Army of Northern Virginia.

The next year saw a series of savage battles in what is called the Overland Campaign. Grant had come to believe that the way to defeat the Confederacy was to keep constant pressure on Lee's army rather than to capture its cities. Grant wanted to wear down the Southern troops in battle after battle.

At that time, the North had a stronger economy than the South. This meant that Grant could easily replace the

Grant's victory at Chattanooga allowed the Union army to invade the lower South.

More than 170,000 African-American soldiers aided the Union war effort.

men and supplies lost in battle. When Lee lost soldiers or weapons, however, he had a hard time replacing them.

Tens of thousands of soldiers died during the Overland Campaign and Grant was called a "butcher" for letting it happen. It was the only way to win, though.

On the morning of April 9, 1865, Lee realized "there is nothing left for me to do but to go and see

General Grant." Grant had been bothered by a headache for days. It quickly disappeared when he got Lee's message of surrender. The two generals met in the little Virginia settlement of Appomattox Court House, and the bloody Civil War was over.

April 9, 1865, was not the first time U.S. Grant and Robert E. Lee met; they knew each other from the Mexican War.

The White House

★ ★ ★

The Civil War had torn the United States apart. When the war ended, the country needed a strong leader. Abraham Lincoln, a man who could make tough decisions and get things done, was shot just five days after Lee's surrender. Lincoln died early the next morning on April 15, 1865, and Vice President Andrew Johnson became president.

Andrew Johnson

Johnson, a Democrat, lacked Lincoln's gift for reaching out to his political enemies. A group of Republican congressmen called "Radical Republicans,"

John Wilkes Booth shot President Lincoln in Ford's Theater, in Washington, D.C.

A political banner supporting the Democratic candidate for president, Horatio Seymour, and his running mate, Francis P. Blair

led by Thaddeus Stevens of Pennsylvania and Charles Sumner of Massachusetts, wanted to punish the Southern states for starting the war. Johnson was more interested in quickly bringing those states back into the Union. The struggle over how to treat the Southern states led to Johnson's near removal from office.

In 1868, the Republicans turned to war hero Ulysses Grant to lead their party to the White House. Grant's running mate was Congressman Schuyler Colfax of Indiana. They ran against Democrat Horatio Seymour, a former New

York governor, and Francis P. Blair Jr., a former Missouri congressman.

Grant campaigned quietly, letting other people convince the voters that he should be president. In the end, Grant won twenty-six states to Seymour's eight. But the popular vote was closer: 3,013,650 to 2,708,744.

As soon as he was elected, Grant showed how new he was to politics. For instance, he chose his **cabinet** without talking to other Republican leaders. Grant brought two generals to his cabinet: John Rawlins as secretary of war, and Jacob Cox as secretary of the interior. Rawlins, Grant's closest friend, was honest and intelligent. However, Rawlins was dead of tuberculosis, a lung disease, by September 1869. Had he lived, Rawlins might have played an important part in Grant's presidency.

Major General Jacob Cox

Probably Grant's best cabinet choice was Hamilton Fish for secretary of state. Fish was a wealthy New Yorker who had served in Congress two decades earlier. He would turn out to be one of the greatest **diplomats** in U.S. history. Grant's cabinet was rounded out with Attorney General E. Rockwood Hoar; Secretary of the Treasury George Boutwell; Postmaster General John Creswell; and Secretary of the Navy George Robeson.

In his first speech as president, Grant said little about national issues. But he did talk about his interest in helping "the original occupants of this land," the

A woodcut showing President Grant meeting with his cabinet

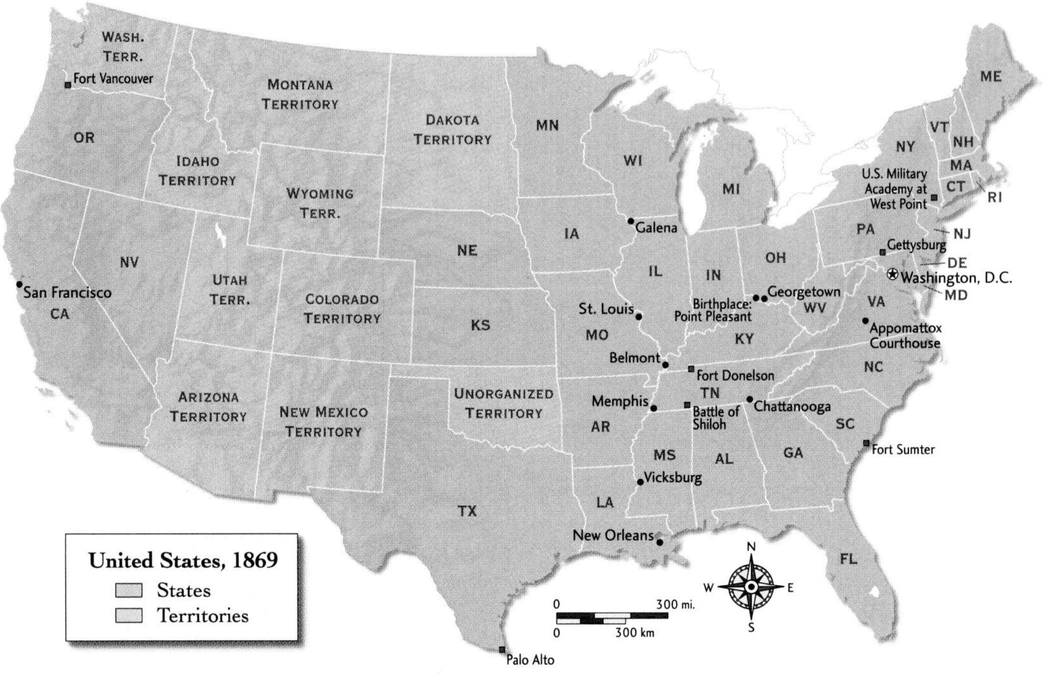

Native Americans. In fact, he named a Seneca Indian and army friend, Ely Parker, to be in charge of Indian affairs.

Conflicts between Indians and white settlers moving west were common. In their attempts to defend their land and their way of life, the Indians

Ely Parker ▸

sometimes attacked settlers. The government sent in the U.S. Army to protect the settlers. In trying to get the Indians out of the way, U.S. troops could be brutal.

Grant thought that if Native Americans could learn white people's ways, it would reduce warfare between the two cultures. In 1869, he called for moving more Indians to **reservations.** There they would learn about white culture and white people's farming methods.

However, reservations were often located on dry, infertile land. It was difficult to farm or make a living on a reservation. As a result, many Indians became completely dependent on the government. They weren't

Fights between Native Americans and whites were common.

Hundreds of thousands of Native Americans were rounded up and sent to reservations against their will.

interested in Grant's idea of becoming American citizens. Despite Grant's efforts, the slaughter of the Indians continued while he was in office.

As president, one of Grant's biggest challenges was trying to ensure the safety and rights of former slaves in the South. After the Civil War, Grant kept U.S. troops stationed in the South to make sure that black men were allowed to vote. He was also in favor of the Fifteenth **Amendment** to the Constitution, which **guarantees** that right.

Hiram Revels

In 1870, Hiram Revels of Mississippi became the first black man elected to the U.S. Senate. But in practice, the freedom of blacks in the South didn't last long. Many Southern whites joined a secret organization called the Ku Klux Klan. The Klan terrorized blacks. Its members used

The Ku Klux Klan was notorious for its hooded members and its campaign of violence against blacks.

This political cartoon depicts Grant defending the Union by attacking the Ku Klux Klan.

violence to keep blacks from voting.

To try and stop the Klan violence, Congress passed the Force Acts. These acts gave Grant the power to send U.S. troops to the South to protect blacks. He used that power only once, however. He thought white Americans were tired of fighting. He did not believe they would support sending troops to the South. He feared it might start another war. It would be almost a century before African-Americans in the South had the same rights as whites.

Grant and others believed that freed slaves might be better off if they lived somewhere else. The Dominican Republic, a small island nation in the Caribbean Sea, offered itself for sale to the United States. Grant wanted to buy it. His plan was then to encourage African-Americans to move there—most of the Dominican Republic's citizens also were black. But the Dominican Republic, which was then called Santo Domingo, was very poor. It was not clear what its position would be within the United States. Grant spent much of his first term trying to sell this plan to Congress but he found little support for it.

Grant had greater success in some of his dealings with other countries. For instance, Secretary of State Hamilton Fish worked out an important deal with Britain. During the Civil War, British shipyards had built some Confederate warships. This made the deadly war last longer. The U.S. government argued that Britain should pay damages. In 1871, Great Britain and the United States agreed to have a five-man international panel of judges settle the conflict. The panel decided that Britain should pay the United States $15.5 million in damages. Because of Fish's careful dealings with Britain, the two powerful countries settled the dispute without going to war.

The Joint High Commission met in Washington, D.C., to settle the dispute between Great Britain and the United States. Hamilton Fish (far left) was able to bring the conflict to a peaceful end.

This was one of the brightest moments of Grant's administration. Much of his eight years in office was tainted by scandal.

In 1869, wealthy businessmen Jay Gould and James Fisk bought up as much gold as possible. They wanted to make gold scarce and drive up its price. They then planned to make a fortune by selling gold to banks and businesses at high prices. Only the U.S. government had enough gold to stop their plan. Gould and Fisk used Grant's brother-in-law Abel Rathbone Corbin to persuade Grant to keep government gold off the market.

When Grant realized what was going on, he had the secretary of the treasury sell government gold. This

Jay Gould

The country panicked ▸ when many banks closed on Black Friday.

brought the price down. But Gould and Fisk's scheme had already done its damage. Many banks failed on September 24, 1869, a day that became known as Black Friday.

▲ *Horace Greeley did not win the presidency, but shaped American history through his influential newspaper, the* New York Tribune.

Despite such scandals, Grant ran for reelection in 1872. Black Republicans and working people saw Grant as their man. He ran against newspaper publisher Horace Greeley. Greeley was supported by Democrats and some Republicans who didn't like Grant's policies. Grant won the election, winning by a larger margin than he had four years earlier.

Though Grant may have thought of himself as a workingman, his policies seldom favored workers. Under Grant, the Republican Party began to develop

An 1869 American greenback, front and back

into a party that favored the business world.

During the Civil War, the U.S. government had issued paper money called **greenbacks**. The government printed so many greenbacks that they amounted to more than the gold that the government held in reserve. This lowered the value of the greenbacks, so that a $1 greenback was worth less than a $1 gold coin. This helped farmers and laborers who owed money, because they could pay back their debts with less valuable money.

But wealthy people did not want any money used that wasn't backed up by gold reserves. Grant sided with them, and the government began getting rid of some of the greenbacks.

The poor fell upon hard times when Grant sided with the rich in the greenbacks debate.

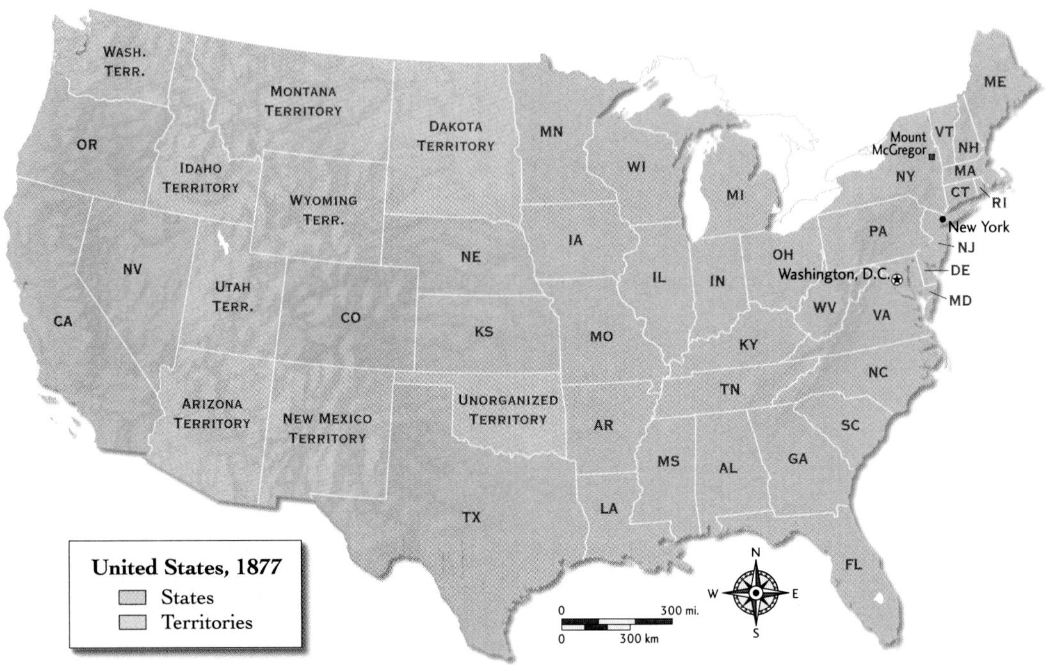

Grant's second term saw the beginning of the country's worst economic depression ever. It began in 1873 with the failure of Jay Cooke & Co., a banking firm. The depression lasted several years. At the time, the United States had no programs to help people who could not find work. Keeping the less valuable greenbacks would have helped farmers and laborers. It was a difficult time for the people who helped elect Grant.

Another dark hour of Grant's presidency became known as the Whiskey Ring scandal. Treasury officials were being paid to give liquor makers big tax breaks.

Grant's close friend and secretary, Orville Babcock, may have been involved. Grant refused to believe it at first. Once again, he had been betrayed by someone he trusted.

This had happened time and again. His administration's achievements were often overshadowed by such dark moments.

This cartoon mocks Grant's second term in office for its seemingly endless string of scandals.

Life After the White House

★ ★ ★

Grant left office after two terms. Many Republicans had seen enough of their war hero, but Grant was still popular with the public. In the minds of many people, he was still "the General." In May 1877, he and Julia left on a two-year world tour. They saw the beauty of ancient Egypt and met the Chinese emperor. Grant was amazed and touched when throngs of people turned out to see him in Great Britain. They cheered him as a great general and a hero.

Back home, Grant once again had to figure out a way to support himself and his family. Unfortunately, Grant's business luck followed its usual pattern. He was hired to be president of a Mexican railroad company, but the railroad went out of business. Grant then invested all his savings—about $100,000—in the banking firm of Grant & Ward, which was owned by his son Ulysses Jr. and a man named Ferdinand Ward. Ward turned out to be dishonest, the bank failed, and Ulysses Grant was penniless once again.

Grant began writing magazine articles about his war experiences. Then he decided to write his memoirs. By that time, Grant was suffering from throat cancer. Still, he worked tirelessly on his book.

In June 1885, the Grants moved to Mount McGregor, New York. People who passed by his house often saw the general resting on his front porch. Ulysses S. Grant died on July 23, 1885. He was sixty-three years old.

Grant's memoirs were published at the suggestion of Mark Twain, a close friend of Grant's.

He had finished his memoirs just one week earlier. They were a great success, and are still considered an outstanding work of military history. Grant's body lies in a tomb in New York City called the General Grant National Memorial. His wife Julia, who died in 1902, is buried by his side.

The tomb of Ulysses S. Grant, Civil War hero and eighteenth president of the United States

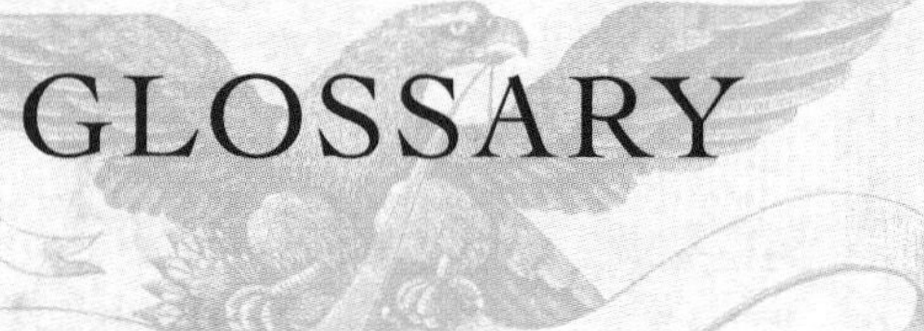

GLOSSARY

amendment—a change made in a law or a legal document

cabinet—a president's group of advisers

diplomats—people who represent their government in a foreign country

forsaken—abandoned

greenbacks—paper money issued by the U.S. government

guarantees—makes sure of; promises

immediate—now; at once

memoirs—a life story

regiment—a military group made up of several battalions

reservations—large areas of land set aside for Native Americans

surrendered—gave up

unconditional—unlimited; absolute

ULYSSES S. GRANT'S LIFE AT A GLANCE

★ ★ ★

PERSONAL

Nickname:	Unconditional Surrender Grant
Birth date:	April 27, 1822
Birthplace:	Point Pleasant, Ohio
Father's name:	Jesse Root Grant
Mother's name:	Hannah Simpson Grant
Education:	Graduated from U.S. Military Academy at West Point, New York, in 1843
Wife's name:	Julia Boggs Dent Grant
Married:	August 22, 1848
Children:	Frederick Dent Grant (1850–1912); Ulysses Simpson Grant (1852–1929); Ellen (Nellie) Wrenshall Grant (1855–1922); Jesse Root Grant (1858–1934)
Died:	July 23, 1885, in Mount McGregor, New York
Buried:	General Grant National Memorial in New York City

PUBLIC

Occupation before presidency:	Soldier
Occupation after presidency:	Businessman, writer
Military service:	First lieutenant during the Mexican War, lieutenant general in charge of all Union forces during the Civil War
Other government positions:	None
Political party:	Republican
Vice presidents:	Schuyler Colfax (1869–1873), Henry Wilson (1873–1875)
Dates in office:	March 4, 1869–March 3, 1877
Presidential opponents:	Horatio Seymour (Democrat), 1868; Horace Greeley (Democrat), 1872
Number of votes (Electoral College):	3,013,650 of 5,722,394 (214 of 294), 1868; 3,598,235 of 6,432,996 (286 of 366), 1872
Writings:	*Personal Memoirs of U.S. Grant* (1885–1886)

Ulysses S. Grant's Cabinet

Secretary of state:
Elihu B. Washburne (1869)
Hamilton Fish (1869–1877)

Secretary of the treasury:
George S. Boutwell (1869–1873)
William A. Richardson (1873–1874)
Benjamin H. Bristow (1874–1876)
Lot M. Morrill (1876–1877)

Secretary of war:
John A. Rawlins (1869)
William T. Sherman (1869)
William W. Belknap (1869–1876)
Alphonso Taft (1876)
James D. Cameron (1876–1877)

Attorney general:
Ebenezer R. Hoar (1869–1870)
Amos T. Akerman (1870–1871)
George H. Williams (1871–1875)
Edwards Pierrepont (1875–1876)
Alphonso Taft (1876–1877)

Postmaster general:
John A. J. Creswell (1869–1874)
James W. Marshall (1874)
Marshall Jewell (1874–1876)
James N. Tyner (1876–1877)

Secretary of the navy:
Adolph E. Borie (1869)
George M. Robeson (1869–1877)

Secretary of the interior:
Jacob D. Cox (1869–1870)
Columbus Delano (1870–1875)
Zachariah Chandler (1875–1877)

ULYSSES S. GRANT'S LIFE AND TIMES

★ ★ ★

GRANT'S LIFE

1822 April 27, Grant is born in Point Pleasant, Ohio (below)

WORLD EVENTS

1820

1820 Susan B. Anthony, a leader of the American woman suffrage movement, is born

1821 Central American countries gain independence from Spain

1823 Mexico becomes a republic

1829 The first practical sewing machine (above) is invented by French tailor Barthélemy Thimonnier

GRANT'S LIFE				WORLD EVENTS
		1830	1833	Great Britain abolishes slavery
			1836	Texans defeat Mexican troops at San Jacinto after a deadly battle at the Alamo
			1837	American banker J. P. Morgan is born
Attends U.S. Military Academy at West Point	1839–1843	1840	1840	Auguste Rodin, famous sculptor of *The Thinker,* is born
Joins the command of General Zachary Taylor in Texas and fights in the Mexican War	1845–1846			
August 22, marries Julia Dent	1848		1848	*The Communist Manifesto,* by German writer Karl Marx (above), is widely distributed
		1850		
Is stationed on the West Coast	1852		1852	American Harriet Beecher Stowe publishes *Uncle Tom's Cabin*
Leaves the army	1854			

GRANT'S LIFE

Rejoins the army as a colonel at the start of the Civil War — 1861

Becomes lieutenant general of the Union army — 1864

Presidential Election Results:

		Popular Votes	Electoral Votes
1868	Ulysses S. Grant	3,013,650	214
	Horatio Seymour	2,708,744	80

1860

WORLD EVENTS

1858 — English scientist Charles Darwin (below) presents his theory of evolution

1865 — *Tristan and Isolde,* by German composer Richard Wagner, opens in Munich

Lewis Carroll writes *Alice's Adventures in Wonderland*

1868 — Louisa May Alcott publishes *Little Women*

GRANT'S LIFE

1869 Tries to convince the Senate that the United States should buy the Dominican Republic; the Senate does not agree

September 24, a day known as Black Friday; wealthy businessmen Jay Gould (left) and James Fisk try to corner the gold market, and many banks fail

1870 Grant signs the Force Acts, approving the use of military power to enforce the rights of African-Americans

1871 A five-judge panel decides that Great Britain will pay for some of the damages caused by British-made ships during the Civil War

1873 The Credit Mobilier scandal reveals that many government officials were bribed

Several major banks fail, starting the Panic of 1873

1870

WORLD EVENTS

1869 The periodic table of elements is invented

The transcontinental railroad across the United States is completed (below)

1870 John D. Rockefeller founds the Standard Oil Company

Presidential Election Results:		*Popular Votes*	*Electoral Votes*
1872	*Ulysses S. Grant*	*3,598,235*	*286*
	*Horace Greeley**	*2,834,761*	
	Thomas A. Hendricks		*42*
	B. Gratz Brown		*18*
	Charles J. Jenkins		*2*
	David Davis		*1*

**Died before electoral votes cast; votes divided among four minor candidates*

GRANT'S LIFE			WORLD EVENTS
Grant's daughter Nellie is married at the White House	1874		
The Whiskey Ring scandal is uncovered, revealing that some tax collectors had accepted money to give tax breaks to liquor makers	1875		
Secretary of War William W. Belknap resigns because of charges of accepting bribes	1876	1876	The Battle of the Little Big Horn is a victory for Native Americans defending their homes in the West against General George Custer (above) Alexander Graham Bell uses the first telephone to speak to his assistant, Thomas Watson
Grant tours the world with his wife	1877–1879	1877	German inventor Nikolaus A. Otto works on what will become the internal combustion engine for automobiles

GRANT'S LIFE

WORLD EVENTS

1879 Electric lights are invented

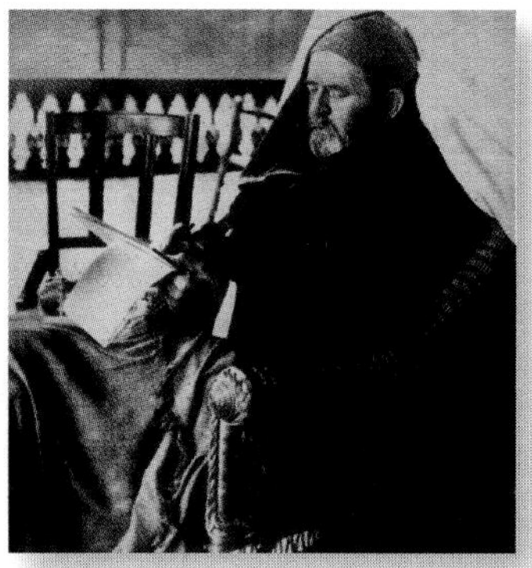

1880

1882 Thomas Edison builds a power station

1884 Mark Twain (right) publishes *The Adventures of Huckleberry Finn*

Writes memoirs; July 23, dies of throat cancer 1885

1886 President Grover Cleveland dedicates the Statue of Liberty in New York

Bombing in Haymarket Square, Chicago, due to labor unrest (below)

UNDERSTANDING ULYSSES S. GRANT AND HIS PRESIDENCY

★ ★ ★

IN THE LIBRARY

Archer, Jules. *A House Divided: The Lives of Ulysses S. Grant and Robert E. Lee.* New York: Scholastic Paperbacks, 1997.

Fitz-Gerald, Christine. *Julia Dent Grant.* Danbury, Conn.: Children's Press, 1998.

O'Shey, Tim, and Arthur Meier Schlesinger. *Ulysses S. Grant: Military Leader and President.* Broomall, Pa.: Chelsea House, 2001.

ON THE WEB

U.S. Grant Memorial
http://saints.css.edu/mkelsey/marq.html
To read about and view the U.S. Grant Memorial in Washington, D.C.

U.S. Grant Photo Gallery
http://www.mscomm.com/~ulysses/page150.html
To view portraits of President Grant

Ulysses S. Grant Chronology
http://www.lib.siu.edu/projects/usgrant/grant2.htm
To follow Grant's life, year by year

Ulysses S. Grant Network
http://saints.css.edu/mkelsey/gppg.html
To read about Grant's life as a general and as the president of the United States

GRANT HISTORIC SITES ACROSS THE COUNTRY

Ulysses S. Grant National Historic Site
7400 Grant Road
Saint Louis, MO 63123
314/842-3298
To visit the site of Grant's estate, which honors his life, military career, and political career

Ulysses S. Grant Homestead
217 East Grant Avenue
Georgetown, OH 45121
937/378-4222
937/378-3760
To visit Grant's boyhood home

Grant's Farm
10501 Gravois Road
Saint Louis, MO 63123
314/843-1700
To visit a wildlife preserve, part of which once belonged to Grant

Grant Birthplace New Richmond Historical Society
1591 State Route 232
Point Pleasant, OH 45153
513/553-4911
To visit the small cottage where Grant was born

Ulysses S. Grant Home State Historic Site
500 Bouthillier Street
P.O. Box 333
Galena, IL 61036
815/777-0248
To visit Grant's home in Galena, Illinois

Grant Cottage State Historic Site
P.O. Box 990
Saratoga Springs, NY 12866
518/587-8277
To visit Grant's summer vacation cottage

THE U.S. PRESIDENTS

(Years in Office)

★ ★ ★

1. **George Washington** (March 4, 1789-March 3, 1797)
2. **John Adams** (March 4, 1797-March 3, 1801)
3. **Thomas Jefferson** (March 4, 1801-March 3, 1809)
4. **James Madison** (March 4, 1809-March 3, 1817)
5. **James Monroe** (March 4, 1817-March 3, 1825)
6. **John Quincy Adams** (March 4, 1825-March 3, 1829)
7. **Andrew Jackson** (March 4, 1829-March 3, 1837)
8. **Martin Van Buren** (March 4, 1837-March 3, 1841)
9. **William Henry Harrison** (March 6, 1841-April 4, 1841)
10. **John Tyler** (April 6, 1841-March 3, 1845)
11. **James K. Polk** (March 4, 1845-March 3, 1849)
12. **Zachary Taylor** (March 5, 1849-July 9, 1850)
13. **Millard Fillmore** (July 10, 1850-March 3, 1853)
14. **Franklin Pierce** (March 4, 1853-March 3, 1857)
15. **James Buchanan** (March 4, 1857-March 3, 1861)
16. **Abraham Lincoln** (March 4, 1861-April 15, 1865)
17. **Andrew Johnson** (April 15, 1865-March 3, 1869)
18. Ulysses S. Grant (March 4, 1869-March 3, 1877)
19. **Rutherford B. Hayes** (March 4, 1877-March 3, 1881)
20. **James Garfield** (March 4, 1881-Sept 19, 1881)
21. **Chester Arthur** (Sept 20, 1881-March 3, 1885)
22. **Grover Cleveland** (March 4, 1885-March 3, 1889)
23. **Benjamin Harrison** (March 4, 1889-March 3, 1893)
24. **Grover Cleveland** (March 4, 1893-March 3, 1897)
25. **William McKinley** (March 4, 1897-September 14, 1901)
26. **Theodore Roosevelt** (September 14, 1901-March 3, 1909)
27. **William Howard Taft** (March 4, 1909-March 3, 1913)
28. **Woodrow Wilson** (March 4, 1913-March 3, 1921)
29. **Warren G. Harding** (March 4, 1921-August 2, 1923)
30. **Calvin Coolidge** (August 3, 1923-March 3, 1929)
31. **Herbert Hoover** (March 4, 1929-March 3, 1933)
32. **Franklin D. Roosevelt** (March 4, 1933-April 12, 1945)
33. **Harry S. Truman** (April 12, 1945-January 20, 1953)
34. **Dwight D. Eisenhower** (January 20, 1953-January 20, 1961)
35. **John F. Kennedy** (January 20, 1961-November 22, 1963)
36. **Lyndon B. Johnson** (November 22, 1963-January 20, 1969)
37. **Richard M. Nixon** (January 20, 1969-August 9, 1974)
38. **Gerald R. Ford** (August 9, 1974-January 20, 1977)
39. **James Earl Carter** (January 20, 1977-January 20, 1981)
40. **Ronald Reagan** (January 20, 1981-January 20, 1989)
41. **George H. W. Bush** (January 20, 1989-January 20, 1993)
42. **William Jefferson Clinton** (January 20, 1993-January 20, 2001)
43. **George W. Bush** (January 20, 2001-)

INDEX

★ ★ ★

ABOUT THE AUTHOR

Jean Kinney Williams lives and writes in Cincinnati, Ohio. Her nonfiction books for children include *Matthew Henson: Polar Adventurer* and a series of books about American religions. She is also the author of *The Pony Express* and *African-Americans in the Colonies.*